THE BENCH

Keir McAllister

Keir McAllister is a stand-up comic and writer. He is a regular headliner at some of the UK's top comedy clubs and festivals. He has also supported the likes of Tom Stade, Stewart Francis and Rory Bremner on tour.

Keir writes for many top comics and has a number of TV / radio credits, including *Live at The Apollo, Stand Up for the Week, Mock the Week, 8 Out of 10 Cats, Breaking the News, The Good, the Bad and the Unexpected* and many more. He has created a string of acclaimed festival shows with other comedians, including the 2015 award-winning *Aye Right? How No?* and the 2012 sell-out show, *Keir McAllister and Vladimir McTavish: Look at the State of Scotland*.

A two-time winner of 'Best Writer' at the Scottish Comedy Awards, Keir has a number of plays under his belt: *Hindsight*, which premiered at the Assembly Rooms during the Edinburgh Fringe in 2013, and went on to four special performances in HMP Barlinnie before returning for the Glasgow International Comedy Festival in 2014 at the Oran Mor; 2014's *A Split Decision*, written in verse, about the Scottish referendum, and 2015's acclaimed *The Last Laugh,* which debuted at the Edinburgh Fringe and went on to tour theatres across Scotland.

Keir lives in Edinburgh with his wife, comedian and presenter Jay Lafferty.

THE BENCH

by Keir McAllister

JOSEF WEINBERGER PLAYS

LONDON

THE BENCH
First published in 2019
by Josef Weinberger Ltd
12-14 Mortimer Street, London W1T 3JJ
www.josef-weinberger.com / plays@jwmail.co.uk

ISBN: 978 0 85676 377 9

THE BENCH was first presented as a co-production between Gilded Balloon and Watch This Space Productions at The Gilded Balloon Basement Theatre, Edinburgh on 17th June 2018 with the following cast:

SANDY .... Paul Sneddon

JOE .... Keir McAllister

Designed & Stage Managed by Jay Lafferty
Directed by Jojo Sutherland

The same cast then presented the play at The Stand Comedy Club, Edinburgh on 21st July 2018, before returning to *The Gilded Balloon* at Rose Theatre for The Edinburgh International Fringe from 1st–26th August 2018.

CHARACTERS

SANDY
a man in his late 60s

JOE
a man in his 30s / 40s

SETTING

An isolated public bench at a scenic spot

Time: The present

AUTHOR'S NOTE

The action takes place over 9 days. I hesitate to call them scenes as they flow into one another and I want to leave how time passes as open to creative interpretation. Recorded or live music can be used to intersect the days and as a soundtrack over the top of the first three days, which have no dialogue. In the original production, the track *In Metaphor, Solace* (Luke Howard , *Open Heart Story, 2018*) was used in between all days except for at the end of Day 7, when the first few bars of *Fists of Fury* (Kamasi Washington, *Heaven and Earth*, Young Turks Recordings, 2018) were used instead. A sound effect of a peaceful country setting was also used at the end.

That which we are capable of feeling, we are capable of saying.

Cervantes

For my wife, Jay, who makes all things possible . . . x

Day 1

A bench sits on the stage. There is a brass plaque on it.

SANDY enters. He carefully arranges some flowers on the bench. Tends to to it. Touches it tenderly, then leaves. Beat.

JOE enters – he is dressed for work and wears a work lanyard with ID card. He is visibly agitated. He approaches the bench and clumsily sits on it, disturbing the laid flowers in the process. He hunts through his pocket for something. Can't find it. Has to stand up again and look through his pockets, becoming more agitated as he does so. He finally finds what he's looking for. A couple of blister packs of pills. He tries to get the pills out of the pack but fails in his agitation. He sits there in silence . . . the silence takes him. He relaxes . . . We watch his agitation go and then JOE starts to cry – tears of relief and exhaustion. JOE pulls himself together. Stands up – lingers for a second then walks away more confident, sure and relaxed.

Day 2

SANDY enters with more flowers.

He immediately notices the original flowers seem to have been disturbed. This annoys and agitates him. He looks round for a culprit. He then tends to the flowers and adds the additional flowers that he has brought. He fusses around the bench, and then, annoyed, exits.

Day 3

JOE enters. He is more relaxed and seems keen to be there. He goes to sit down on the bench and notices the flowers. He reads the plaque and then gently moves the flowers so he can sit down. He is lost in his thoughts as SANDY enters. Music fades.

SANDY   Having a seat?

(*Beat.*)

Taking a seat to yourself there . . . ?

JOE	Aye . . . yes . . .
SANDY	Were those flowers there when you sat down?
JOE	Sorry? . . . Eh . . .
SANDY	The flowers there – did you move them?
JOE	I've just got here, mate . . .
SANDY	And when you got here . . . where were the flowers? Were they in their current state of situ?
JOE	Mate – I just want a seat – I didn't see anyone touch the flowers?
SANDY	I did not ask if you had witnessed anyone touching the flowers – I asked if you yourself had touched them . . . .
JOE	Look mate – the flowers are there – they look good to me – I just sat down – I just want 5 minutes' peace – then I'll be gone . . .

(*Beat.*)

SANDY	They look good to you?
JOE	What?
SANDY	The flowers – you think they look good?
JOE	They look great mate . . .

(*Beat.*)

SANDY	Five minutes' peace . . .
JOE	What?

SANDY	What?
JOE	I thought you said something.
SANDY	It was just what you said.
JOE	What *I* said? What did *I* say?
SANDY	*You just want five minutes' peace?*
JOE	I did say that.
SANDY	Five minutes' peace is all you wanted.
JOE	. . . Then I'll be gone . . .
SANDY	. . . Five minutes' peace.
JOE	Yes.
SANDY	A man or woman's peace should not be interrupted, I agree.
JOE	I'm glad . . .
SANDY	Peace is sacrosanct, it is our right as human beings . . . a *human right,* if you will . . .
JOE	. . . Couldn't agree more.
SANDY	And therefore it is our moral obligation, as emotional sentient human beings to respect each others' peace – would you also agree?
JOE	What?
SANDY	That is a thing we should do – isn't it? We should strive not to disturb the peace – people who are at peace . . . those who are resting at peace, they, above all, should be respected?
JOE	Yes – absolutely . . .

SANDY   So why did you move those flowers?!

JOE   What?

SANDY   . . . I'm just wondering why a man such as
               yourself, who, as we have just established,
               regards his right to peace so highly . . . as you
               should . . . nothing wrong with that . . . but why
               then you would be so recklessly cavalier with
               the peace of others? . . .

JOE   What are you talking about? – I just want a seat,
               mate . . . I just came here for a seat . . .

SANDY   That is your interpretation of events . . .

JOE   And what's yours?

SANDY   That you swanned in here – *strode,* I would say
               – you *strode* in here – to this place – without
               so much as a pause for thought, no reverence
               at all, with an air of – may I say – *impetuous
               arrogance,* you swipe the flowers – carefully
               arranged blooms of remembrance from their
               resting place then you have the cheek to
               begin an aggressive verbal assault on me for
               disturbing *your* peace . . .

JOE   . . . I have not verbally aggressively assaulted
               anyone . . . .

SANDY   . . . As the attacker, your opinion on the ferocity
               of your hate speech is moot . . .

JOE   . . . The attacker . . . ? I haven't attacked you,
               mate – I just want to sit for five minutes – here
               – not bother anyone – I'm not going to touch
               the flowers – I'm not going to attack you – I'm
               not even going to speak to you mate – no-one is
               attacking or assaulting anyone . . . if we got off
               on the wrong foot – I'm sorry about that – all I
               wanted . . . I just wanted to be left alone . . .

SANDY	So now you're trying to force me to leave? . . .
JOE	. . . Look, mate . . . would you calm down? – I'm not trying to get you to leave – I don't care what you do . . .
SANDY	Yes, it's clear you care very little for other people around you . . .
JOE	Mate, look – you don't know me . . . I'm beginning to get annoyed . . .
SANDY	. . . Oh no! Not that, surely . . . you're going to get annoyed, are you? *You* are getting annoyed? (*Addresses imaginary crowd.*) We can't be having that . . . why didn't you say earlier? I had no idea . . . quick, everybody, everybody come out from your houses, gather in the town square – (*To* JOE.) What's your name?

(SANDY *grabs the lanyard around* JOE'S *neck and looks at his name.*)

	. . . People, Joe here is about to get annoyed . . . I know I know . . . but it's too late for pointing fingers . . . that's the reality we are living in . . . no point denying that . . . now what are we going to do about this situation? Because we all know that the things that upset Joe here . . . Joe's level of annoyance . . . is of paramount importance to the functioning of this universe –
JOE	. . . Who are you talking to . . . ?
SANDY	Nobody, Joe, and do you know why I'm talking to nobody, Joe? Because nobody cares whether you're annoyed or not . . .
JOE	What is going on here, mate? What is this about? Because I have done nothing to you . . . nothing . . .

SANDY   . . . Nothing? Nothing, you say?

JOE   Not a thing – am I saying it too fast? – I came in
             here, I sat down . . .

SANDY   . . . Liar!

JOE   What are you talking about? That's what
             happened . . . that's exactly what happened . . .

SANDY   . . . Liar! . . . Liar! . . .

JOE   . . . Mate, if you call me a liar once more, I'll . . .

SANDY   . . . You'll what? Finish that sentence . . . what
             will you do? . . .

JOE   . . . I'm not looking for a fight – now I don't
             know if you have problems, maybe you're just
             having a bad day, but I swear to you – I walked
             in here and I sat on this bench . . . .

SANDY   Liar, liar, liar, liarrrr!

JOE   What the . . . what is wrong with you?! – Stop
             calling me a liar . . . I am not lying . . .

SANDY   . . . You did not just walk up here and just
             casually sit down on this bench – that is a lie
             – it is a reckless misrepresentation of the truth
             – what you did – the exact sequence of events
             that happened was in fact that you walked
             in here – *moved the flowers* . . . and then sat
             down – is that not true?

JOE   . . . I . . .

SANDY   Did you move the flowers?

JOE   . . . Look . . .

SANDY   . . . Did you move the flowers? Simple yes or
           no?

JOE   . . . Why are you . . . ?

SANDY   . . . Okay, let me try another way – were the
           flowers in that position when you arrived
           here? . . .

JOE   . . . Man . . . all I wanted was five minutes'
           peace . . .

SANDY   . . . Just a yes or no . . . did you move the
           flowers? . . .

JOE   . . . Will you stop . . .

SANDY   (*Over the top of* JOE's *attempts to interrupt.*) . . .
           Did you move the flowers? . . .Yes or no? . . .
           Very simple question? . . . Very simple answer .
           . . . were the flowers moved? . . . Yes . . . . how
           were they moved? . . . The wind? . . . Don't
           think so . . . so it must have been a person who
           moved the flowers, and since there's only you
           and I in the vicinity . . . then call me Sherlock
           Holmes, but I'm thinking . . .

JOE   . . . I moved the flowers! (*Beat.*) It was me, I
           confess. Everybody – the madness is over – I
           moved the flaming flowers. I committed the
           heinous crime, I am to blame – I am the botanic
           anti-Christ – invisible people, come from your
           houses – come to the town square – string
           me up, stone me, then behead me because I
           am an evil man – an evil, evil man – who in
           search for five minutes' peace moved a bunch
           of supermarket-bought flowers – not even from
           a proper florist – from one side of a fucking
           bench to the other . . . I deserve punishment –
           how could I have done such a thing? If only I
           had just stayed home and continued to torture
           the puppies in the privacy of my cellar, but

no . . . instead, I have come out into normal
society, in broad daylight, despite my hideous
form and have deliberately, and full of malice,
moved a limp bunch of shitty-looking tulips
three foot to the opposite side of the *public* –
let's not forget that word – *public* – bench – a
bench which I had wrongly assumed had been
provided for the explicit purpose of the seating
of *members of the public* – but no, turns out a
public bench in this town is actually reserved
for the sole purpose of showcasing the only
flowers in the history of flowers that actually
make you sadder than you were before . . . oh,
Gods above, how can I repent for such a cruel
and evil act against mankind? . . .

(*Beat.*)

SANDY   It is not a bench. (*Exits.*)

(JOE *looks after him, annoyed, then leaves.*)

Day 4

SANDY *enters. He has brought even more memorial paraphernalia
and is stood solemnly by the bench.* JOE *enters. He is not
expecting to see* SANDY *and is visibly disappointed when he does.
Sees him. Stops. Turns around. Walks away. Stops. Turns back
to* SANDY. *There is an expensive, extravagant-looking bunch of
flowers on the bench. The old flowers are also still there.*

JOE   Nice flowers . . . (*Beat.*) Those are really
               nice flowers. I'm not being sarcastic. They're
               beautiful. Very nice.

               (SANDY *remains silent and still.*)

               . . . I am sorry . . . about yesterday . . . I'm sorry
               . . . I was upset, you were upset . . . anyway –
               the flowers are very . . . nice . . . and I'm sorry

	. . . about yesterday . . . I didn't mean to offend you . . .
SANDY	You didn't offend me . . .
JOE	. . . upset you, then . . .
SANDY	It takes a lot more than the likes of you to upset the likes of me. Don't you worry about it.
JOE	Fine – I wont . . . (*Beat.*) Look, this is silly – I don't want this to be a thing . . .
SANDY	I thought you wanted your peace, Joe? Your five minutes of precious peace?
JOE	. . . Well exactly, but it's very hard to be at peace when there's a guy lurching about actively hating you . . .
SANDY	I am not hating you. I do not care about you enough to hate you. You do not hate those who are to be pitied . . . and I am just as entitled to be here as you are – perhaps *some* would consider more so . . .
JOE	. . . Pitied . . . and why am I to be pitied?
SANDY	I don't expect you to understand . . . go back to your little peace, Joe . . .
JOE	I can't go back to my peace – you have robbed me of my peace . . . I want to know why I've to be pitied and more so – why you think you have more right than me to be here?
SANDY	I pity you, Joe, because of your ignorance . . . because of your lack of compassion . . . because of your blatant disrespect, Joe, and I did not say *I had more right to be here* – I said, and I quote, *I am just as entitled to be here as*

	you are – perhaps <u>some</u> would consider more so . . .
JOE	Which *some?* Who is *some?* Why – why would *some* consider more so?
SANDY	Many reasons.
JOE	What reasons?
SANDY	Reasons you are not capable of understanding . . .
JOE	I am not doing this with you again . . . I'm not getting drawn in to your . . . petty . . . .
SANDY	. . . I did not start this conversation – you insisted on talking to me with your *nice flower* chat – your opinion of the flowers means nothing to me . . . I was just trying to be polite by responding . . .
JOE	. . . Polite? you? . . . Look, let's just not talk to each other, okay? Let's not talk at all – no speaking . . . right?
SANDY	I didn't want to speak in the first place . . . as I have said . . .
JOE	Good.
SANDY	. . . It was you who . . .
JOE	. . . Right, then – no speaking – as of now . . .
	(*Beat.*)
	. . . And you obviously *do* care about my opinion of the flowers . . .
SANDY	. . . What was that? . . .

JOE	Nothing . . . I just said you obviously do care very much about my opinion of the flowers . . . no point in denying that . . . that's all . . . let's not speak . . .
SANDY	Do I now?
JOE	Shhh.
SANDY	I do not care what you think about the flowers, they are not for you . . . they are not about you . . .
JOE	I think you know you do . . .
SANDY	And how could you possibly hope to think what I think . . .
JOE	So you're saying you don't care about my opinion of your flowers? . . .
SANDY	That's exactly what I'm saying.
JOE	Don't care at all?
SANDY	I care so little about your opinion on anything that I deeply resent having this conversation about not caring about it . . .
JOE	Liar . . .
SANDY	What did you just call me? . . .
JOE	The same thing you called me yesterday when I met you for the first time . . . *Liar* . . .
SANDY	Why is that, then?
JOE	Because you're lying . . . you care – you care very much what I think of your flowers . . . you are lying . . .

SANDY	You dare call me a liar? Tell me what you consider me to be lying about . . .
JOE	Tell me, why would anyone think you are more entitled than me to be here . . . ?
SANDY	I did not say that, that is not what I said . . .
JOE	You implied it.
SANDY	I suggested *some,* not all, that *some* may consider my presence here as more significant than yours . . .
JOE	You've made that clear – *why?* I want to know *why* you think it's okay to think that.
SANDY	I think it's okay to think anything.
JOE	Well I think most normal people would think that it's not okay to think that and it's not okay to think just anything . . .
SANDY	You've clearly put a lot of thought into this . . .
JOE	What do you mean by that?
SANDY	I mean I don't care . . . You're entitled to think whatever you want to think about what I think about your thinking . . .
JOE	. . . Think you . . . thank you . . . but you have not answered my question . . . why would your presence here be considered more significant than mine? The only possible answer to that is that you believe me to be a lesser person than you? . . . Because you consider yourself to be of higher value? . . .
SANDY	Not me – *my purpose* . . . this is futile . . . you are not capable of this level of discussion – I do not believe I am intrinsically of more value than

	you . . . if you weren't such a vulgar idiot you'd understand that . . .
JOE	Listen to yourself . . . all right, then – what is your purpose? Explain to me *your* purpose, because up till now the only purpose you've served is to ensure that *Help the Aged*[1] are getting one less monthly donation from now on . . .
SANDY	Was that a joke . . . ? Are you making jokes? . . .
JOE	I am using levity to displace my anger.
SANDY	. . . Jokes about old people? . . . About *Help the Aged?* . . . Here? . . . You think that's appropriate?
JOE	I'm sorry if I offended you – I am frustrated . . .
SANDY	It takes a lot more than the likes of you to offend the likes of me . . .
JOE	Liar.
SANDY	How dare you call me . . .
JOE	. . . My very presence here offends you, you were offended by me before you even met me. The offence is visibly rising off of you right now . . . like steam off a bull – you couldn't be more offended if I sat here and took a shit on this bench . . .
SANDY	. . . Don't you dare . . .
JOE	. . . I'm not going to . . . I was obviously joking . . .

---

1 'Help the Aged' doesn't exist anymore but it still had the highest recognition with the audience as a reference, which is why we used it. Could be substituted with any charity who work with the elderly.

SANDY   That's you're purpose here? – That's what you're
               here to do – make jokes? – Cause offence? . . .

JOE   You just told me I couldn't possibly cause you
               offence.

SANDY   You haven't – I'm not offended.

JOE   This is your *not-offended* voice, is it?

SANDY   You don't offend me because you can't offend
               me . . . you don't know the meaning of anything
               . . . so how can you offend me? . . .

JOE   What are you talking about – *I don't know the
               meaning of anything?* What a shitty thing to
               say . . .

SANDYl   It's true . . .

JOE   You don't know me . . .

SANDY   I know your type . . .

JOE   And what type am I?

SANDY   I thought we weren't talking . . .

JOE   No – what type am I? what type of person do
               you associate me with? . . .

SANDY   I have no wish to continue this conversation . . .

JOE   Neither do I but we're here now, so out with
               it . . . What *type*? (*Beat.*) Is that how you see
               people, as types? . . . What type of person am I
               to you?

SANDY   . . . The type of person who thinks it's
               appropriate to make jokes about dying at a
               memorial . . . the type of person who moves
               flowers left in tribute then lies about it, the

type of person who has no empathy for others, no respect for the dead and no concern for anything further than ensuring your own selfish needs are met . . . that is your type . . . that is the type of guy you are . . .

JOE   How's that a type? That's not a type of person, that's just your lunatic version of what happened here . . . This is insane – now look – it was not my intention to cause any kind of disrespect to you – I was not being irreverent – this is a public bench for the use of the public. Now if I've been clumsy in any way I apologise, I did not mean to do that . . . do you understand that? . . . I'm not trying to piss you off . . .

SANDY   . . . You couldn't piss me off even if you tried . . .

JOE   In the name of God, would you give it a rest . . .

SANDY   Would you please refrain from blasphemy . . .

JOE   Jesus . . . sorry . . . sorry . . . look, come on, I'm not trying to piss you off, man! Look – can we stop this? Seriously now, look – I'm sorry, okay – stop it now. Right – I've apologised to you – I take full responsibility . . . do you accept my apology?

SANDY   Not necessary. Just go about doing what you were doing . . . whatever that was . . .

JOE   What do you mean – whatever that was? What is wrong with you? You know what I was doing; I was sitting on the fucking bench . . .

SANDY   Now the swearing . . . first jokes – then the blasphemy, now the swearing . . . we all know what's coming next . . .

JOE   Are you real? Am I going mad? Seriously, am I
                hallucinating? Am I the only one who can see
                you? Can I pinch you to make sure you're not a
                projection of my own self-loathing?

SANDY   . . . Threats of violence . . . there it is! You will
                not touch me – what's your name? . . . That
                was a direct threat – I demand you tell me your
                name . . . (*Takes out notepad and pencil.*)

JOE   I'm not actually sure anymore . . .

SANDY   Joe what? Joe – as in Joseph?

                (SANDY *goes to grab the lanyard again but* JOE
                grabs it back.)

JOE   Joe as in fucking Joe.

SANDY   Would you please refrain from swearing? Joe
                what?

JOE   Joe Mc . . . hang on, what do you want to know
                my name for?

SANDY   As custodian of this memorial . . . .

JOE   Custodian . . . how are you a custodian? . . .

SANDY   As custodian . . .

JOE   It's a public bench . . .

SANDY   It is not a bench . . . I paid for the plaque; I
                therefore supervise its upkeep, therefore I am
                the custodian.

JOE   That does not make you the custodian; you paid
                for the plaque, not the whole . . .

SANDY   . . . Memorial.

JOE	. . . Bench. It's a fucking bench, you mad old . . .
SANDY	Ah – name-calling – threats and name-calling – harassment – this is harassment.
JOE	You wont leave *me* alone – how is it harassment? It's no more harassment than this is not a bench . . .
SANDY	It's not a bench. It was a bench – it has now transcended the function of mere bench and taken on a greater purpose.
JOE	Are you telling me this thing here is not a bench? This wooden seat here, placed out for the public to sit on . . . is not a bench? . . .
SANDY	Not any more . . .
JOE	So if we were on a quiz show, if we were on *Pointless?*[2]
SANDY	What's *Pointless?*
JOE	This conversation . . . *The Chase,* then – you must have seen *The Chase* . . . the team have to face the chaser . . . one of them's a big fat guy . . .
SANDY	I never watch these fitness things . . .
JOE	What?
SANDY	Fat folk trying to lose weight, not for me.
JOE	What? Who?
SANDY	The big fat guy
JOE	No, he's the chaser . . .

---

2 *Pointless, The Chase* and *Mastermind* are all running quiz shows on UK television. These can be changed to more culturally-relevant references if required.

SANDY	And are the team fat as well? That's a bit unfair otherwise if he's got to chase them and they're all thin . . .
JOE	. . . No it's not about being fat – it's a quiz show – forget it – *Mastermind*? Have you seen *Mastermind*?
SANDY	No.
JOE	You've not seen *Mastermind*?
SANDY	No.
JOE	You've never seen an episode of *Mastermind*.
SANDY	No.
JOE	Not once, longest-running quiz show on telly, big black chair . . . duh du du duh . . . day do.
SANDY	I told you – no.
JOE	Have you seen any quiz shows at all?
SANDY	I've seen *Celebrity Mastermind*.
JOE	Fuck me – right – so if you were on *Celebrity Mastermind* . . .
SANDY	Would never happen.
JOE	No shit . . . it's hypothetical . . . pretend . . .
SANDY	I can't pretend to be on *Celebrity Mastermind* because I'm not a celebrity, am I? So it would just be *Mastermind*.
JOE	I thought you said you hadn't seen *Mastermind*.
SANDY	I haven't.
JOE	What are you talking about, then?

SANDY	I can't very well pretend to be on *Celebrity Mastermind* if I'm not a celebrity, can I?
JOE	Just pretend you're a celebrity – its not real – you can pretend to be whoever you like.
	(*Beat.*)
SANDY	Oh aye, I could do that, right enough . . . aye . . .
JOE	So you're on *Mastermind.*
SANDY	*Celebrity Mastermind . . .*
JOE	. . . *Celebrity Mastermind,* you're on *Celebrity Mastermind,* and it's the final question of the grand final and there's one point in it . . .
SANDY	As who, though?
JOE	What?
SANDY	Which celebrity?
JOE	It doesn't matter . . . whoever you like . . . so there's one point in it and . . .
SANDY	Moira Stewart[3] . . .
JOE	Okay . . . one point and you've won – you are *Celebrity Mastermind 2018* and then they show you a picture of this object here and they say identify this object – a picture of this here – and to win the game you have to say what it is. What would you say? . . . What answer would you give to win the game?
	(*Beat.*)

---

3 Moira Stewart is a well-known UK newsreader. I picked her because it was such an incongruous person for Sandy to pick. Again can be substituted for a more culturally-relevant celebrity.

SANDY   They don't do picture rounds on *Celebrity
             Mastermind* . . .

JOE   . . . You can't do it, can you?

SANDY   . . . Well I'm not really Moira Stewart . . .

JOE   . . . Not the imaginary game show, *this* . . . *this*
             here . . . you can't do *this* . . . Can't engage
             with me like a normal human being, can't see
             my point of view . . . you don't *want* to see my
             point of view – you want to stand there and be
             offended, that is what you want . . .

SANDY   I want this place to be appropriately respected
             . . . as the custodian of this bench . . .

JOE   You're not a custodian, mate – there's no such
             thing as a *bench custodian,* just like there's no
             such thing as a *lamppost warden,* or a *letterbox
             jannie* . . .

SANDY   I paid for that plaque . . . that plaque is the soul
             of that bench . . .

JOE   I don't give a shit about the plaque, mate – take
             it home with you – stick it on the back of your
             sofa for all I care – this is a public bench and I
             have as much right to be here as you . . .

SANDY   Did I say you didn't have a right to be here? No
             I did not . . .

JOE   You said you have more right than me to
             be here . . . that is what you said . . . at the
             beginning . . .

SANDY   I said *some* – I said *some* might think I had
             more right to be here . . .

JOE   You don't know what you're saying.

SANDY	I know what I am saying – I am very careful with what I say.
JOE	I can prove to you you have no idea what you are saying.
SANDY	Oh, can you? – Go on, then . . .
JOE	You said you don't care what I think about your flowers . . .
SANDY	Correct.
JOE	You admit you said that?
SANDY	I said that.
JOE	Sure? You are a hundred percent sure you said that?
SANDY	Yes I am . . .
JOE	So tell me this – why did you get more expensive flowers today?
SANDY	What?
JOE	Yesterday – I insulted your flowers – I was angry – I said your flowers looked shitty – today – da rah . . . lovely flowers . . .
SANDY	And you think that's because of you? . . .
JOE	Course it's because of me . . . you *wanted* to see me today, to rub my nose in it . . . get a little social revenge . . . since I left you last night . . . this here, this is all you could think about . . . this meeting me here today . . . how you would orchestrate your little psychological drama . . . that's it, isn't it? You've been up all night thinking about me – I've got you bang to rights . . .

SANDY	Exactly what I would expect from someone of your type . . .
JOE	Sorry?
SANDY	Your type, your type, the type that sees a man laying flowers at memorial and thinks it's about him . . . that's exactly your type . . . the lot of you . . . and that is why – that is why *some* might say I have more right to be here than you . . . because I serve a purpose – greater than me . . .
JOE	And what would that be? What you doing here that's so much more worthy than me?
SANDY	I am grieving. That's what I'm doing . . . grieving.

(SANDY *exits, upset and furious,* JOE *is left standing, angry and sorry. He exits, regretful.*)

Day 5

There is now a soft toy and two burning candles on the bench along with the flowers. SANDY *is standing, head bowed, as* JOE *enters.* JOE *is also carrying a huge bunch of flowers.* SANDY *doesn't flinch as* JOE *enters, tentatively puts down the flowers and then awkwardly stands alongside* SANDY *head bowed . . .*

SANDY	(*Beat.*) What are you doing?
JOE	I'm trying to show the proper respect. Look, I'm sorry about yesterday . . . things are a little tense for me at the moment . . . I'm not myself . . . I shouldn't have . . . (*Beat.*) I'm sorry . . . for your loss. (*Reads.*) "To Maggie, forever remembered." . . . She must have been very special . . .
SANDY	You have no idea . . .

JOE	I'm sorry. . . . I'm sorry – I've been a . . . look, can we start again? I mean I don't even know your name . . . (*Beat.*) We got off on the wrong foot. I can't imagine what it must be like to . . . I'm sorry . . . for your loss . . . really I am . . .
SANDY	Sandy. My name is Sandy.
JOE	It's nice to meet you, Sandy . . . I'm Joe.
SANDY	I know that.
JOE	I know you know that – I was just reintroducing myself . . . new start . . . we can talk if you like . . . if that would help . . .
SANDY	And what would we talk about? *Celebrity Mastermind?*
JOE	Anything you like – we could talk about Maggie if you like. Sometimes it helps to talk . . . not that I'd know – just that's what they say, isn't it? . . . Don't bottle it up . . .
SANDY	Who's they? Who says this?
JOE	Everybody says this – I hear it all the time – everyone says it . . . well presumably not everyone – otherwise there'd be no-one to say it to . . . in fact there must be quite a lot of people who go around bottling things up to warrant it being said so often by everyone else . . . it's probably about fifty-fifty – half the world are bottling things up – half the world are telling them not to . . .
SANDY	Is this meant to be helping?
JOE	I'm babbling . . . you make me nervous . . . we don't need to talk . . .
	(*Beat.*)

SANDY	Nice flowers.
JOE	Thank you. I wanted to . . . you know . . . pay due respect . . .
SANDY	Appreciated.
JOE	Did she like it here? . . . I mean – do you mind me asking? . . . I won't if you . . .
SANDY	This was her favourite place . . . this was where I met her . . . this very bench . . .
JOE	I can understand why this is so special to you . . .
SANDY	No you can't. You have no idea. How could you? You never knew her.
JOE	Of course not, I wasn't trying to offend you – I just meant . . . I can understand.
SANDY	What do you understand?
JOE	. . . That this place must be special for you, that you must miss her a lot, that it's difficult and sore . . . maybe I don't understand but I empathise . . . as a human being, God, I can do that, can't I? (*Beat.*) You remember the day you met?
SANDY	Of course I do.
JOE	Was it a day like today?
SANDY	No, it was a much nicer day.
JOE	Obviously, of course, but I mean . . . I don't know . . . I just thought you might like to talk – remember out loud . . . you don't have to . . . we could just sit here in silence . . . say nothing . . . quiet contemplation . . . meditate

on life . . . just stay quiet . . . sitting here . . . in complete silence . . .

SANDY   . . . For crying out loud . . . fine . . . it was a cold day. I was sitting here, just came for a walk, *get five minutes' peace,* and she came up that hill like you did, except she was with some one else . . . she was with Richard . . . and everything changed . . . I fell in love that day . . .

JOE   Sounds like it was a much nicer day.

SANDY   My heart was blown into a million pieces. It was as though I had never seen anything before . . . felt anything . . . been anything until that moment. Isn't it an amazing thing, that you can see the world one way . . . be so sure that the way you see the world is the way the world actually is and then *kaboom* . . . out of the blue, you have this thought . . . something occurs to you that had never occurred to you before and there and then your everything shifts on its axis . . . everything is completely different and you are, from that moment on . . . fundamentally and forever changed . . .

JOE   What did you do?

SANDY   I couldn't do anything. What could I do? I've never been so frightened, bewildered and smitten in all my life. But I couldn't say anything, could I? Not me. I'm very much from the half that bottles it up. When I was born, everyone bottled everything up. Things were a lot tidier then.

JOE   And Maggie? Maggie, what did she do? Did she know?

SANDY   Maggie? In her own way maybe . . .

JOE   What did she do?

SANDY   She just sat there . . . sometimes she would go
             for a wander, sometimes she would just sit in
             the grass, get up and run around for no reason
             and sit back down again . . .

JOE   . . . She sounds . . . fun . . .

SANDY   She was – full of fun – impudent, I guess . . .
             cheeky . . . could always surprise you. Once I
             came up here – wait till you hear this – I could
             hear her, but I couldn't see her – so I'm looking
             around – I can't see her, and then I go further
             into the bushes and she's just standing there,
             quite the thing – licking a fox . . .

JOE   Wait . . . what? . . .

SANDY   . . . And she knew fine what she was doing, but
             she'd look up at you with those big eyes . . .
             wagging her tail with that cheeky grin and she'd
             just bark . . .

JOE   Maggie is a fucking dog?!

SANDY   Aye, of course . . .

JOE   She's not your wife?

SANDY   My wife? No my wife's in the house . . .

JOE   Hang on . . . you said you fell in love that day
             . . . Sandy – I mean I know people care a lot
             about their animals, but this is disturbing . . .

SANDY   Don't be so bloody stupid – I fell in love with
             Richard . . . idiot . . . Maggie was his dog . . . a
             wee Scottie . . .

JOE   Hang on . . . this, this memorial bench is for
             a fucking Scottie dog called Maggie? Do you
             know how insulting that is to most Scottish

people – a *Scottie* dog called *Maggie?!*[4] I bought a £30 bunch of flowers . . . for a fucking dead mutt named after the Queen of the Tories . . . I spent less on my own gran's flowers . . . and she was a Lib Dem . . .

SANDY   Don't you dare swear about her . . . don't you bring shame on that dog – you have no idea what you're talking about – you have no idea . . .

JOE   I've been feeling guilty, I couldn't sleep last night thinking about you and what you must be going through and it turns out you're just an old queen who lost his corgi . . .

SANDY   How dare you? That is homophobic – I will no longer be bullied by your type . . .

JOE   My type? Look at the state of this bench – you'd be mistaken for thinking Princess Diana crashed here . . .

SANDY   You leave her alone as well – she was good to us . . . you're homophobic, that's what this is about . . .

JOE   It's got nothing to do with you being a poof – it's about you being a mad old bastard.

SANDY   There you go again with your homophobic slurs – this is a hate crime . . .

JOE   No – *this* (*Motioning to bench.*) is a hate crime, A hate crime against every poor prick who fancies a seat. You've held me to ransom with

4 This gag is particular to a Scottish audience and the play being placed in Scotland, the joke being that Scotland is notoriously anti-Conservative. If the play is placed elsewhere, then the context of the gag can be changed, e.g. The name of the dog could be changed to Theresa and the line substituted to: *Do you know how insulting that is?* – *Most people around here voted to remain.* Outside of the UK it may be appropriate to change the name of Maggie to a more culturally-appropriate reference.

your *grief* . . . I hardly slept last night thinking about you and it's all for your boyfriend's dog? You want to talk about types? I know your type – a repressed, old, boring fud[5] who is so miserable his only aim in life is to exploit every sadness in this world to his advantage . . . spread the bleak torment around . . .

SANDY   How dare you! You're a homophobe . . . and you're ageist, and as custodian of this bench . . .

JOE   Sandy – you're custodian of hee-haw . . . this is a public bench and from now on I'll be using this bench when I see fit for as long as I see fit in whatever manner I see fit . . . and if my time on this bench is in any way disturbed by you, if you make a single dour comment or passive aggressive remark I swear on the ghost of Lassie, the Littlest Hobo and Scooby-fucking-Doo – I will find where Maggie is buried, dig her up and create my own memorial by shoving what's left of her up your misanthropic arse . . .

           (JOE *storms off.*)

SANDY   Well you can't dig her up cos we cremated her – so get it round you!

           (JOE *then storms back, picks up the flowers and storms off again.*)

Day 6

There is a placard facing away from the audience. The various memorial items from the bench are neatly stacked to the side, SANDY is varnishing the bench from an ancient-looking tin. For the whole of this scene he continues to do that, unless stage directions instruct him otherwise. JOE enters.

5 This, again, is a particularly Scottish insult and can be changed to 'twat'.

JOE

Oh no. Oh no, no, no, no, no . . . you have
got to be kidding me . . . you are taking the
absolute pish now. This is sabotage . . . you are
sabotaging my time on this bench, deliberately
and with malice . . . this is to get back at me
. . . you're a joke . . . I can't believe you've
done this – are you not going to say anything?
. . . Well joke's on you, pal, because I have
a friend on the council . . . in the bench
department . . . and I have a very good lawyer
– who I also know also has an invested interest
in dealing with passive-aggressive, interfering
old . . . I'm going to phone him now, actually
. . . you have no right to do this, this is not
your bench, it is a public bench and this is
tantamount to vandalism . . . so I'm going
to phone my lawyer now . . . do you have
anything to say about that? . . .

(SANDY *stands up, goes into his pocket and
hands* JOE *a piece of paper then goes back to
varnishing . . .)*

"As volunteer custodian of this bench, I have
received written permission, see attached – to
use today for memorial maintenance which
will be carried out in full compliance with all
council safety codes, with every effort taken
to ensure that the least disruption possible is
caused to access of said memorial. However,
we do ask that patrons be tolerant as we
endeavour to carry out the necessary repairs
to ensure the ongoing long-term future of this
poignant tribute to the beautiful Maggie, who
will always be remembered in our hearts . . .
Regards, Sandy, brackets, custodian, end of
brackets" . . .

Ever heard of a full stop? . . . There's murderers
with shorter sentences . . . this means nothing
– the council are not aware of the full context

of this. When my lawyer explains to them that
you are simply a vindictive power freak with
a grudge – things will change, my friend . . .
I'm phoning him now . . . oh and and if you're
doing this in full compliance of council safety
codes – where's your sign, eh? Where's your
wet paint sign? If I sat on that and ruined my
clothes you'd be liable . . . you could get done
for not using the sign alone . . . that could cost
the council thousands . . .

(SANDY *turns over a sign saying "wet paint" with
an arrow pointing towards the bench, which
was lying unseen on the ground.*)

Oh, very good, aye, very good. Did you just
take that down when you saw me coming, did
you? You wanted me to ruin my clothes . . .
look – you've turned that sign round as well . . .
hiding that from me too, were you?

(SANDY *gets up again turns the placard round
and then goes straight back to varnishing. The
sign reads "homophobic prick", with an arrow
pointing toward* JOE.)

Oh – ha ha – you're very pleased with yourself
. . . I can see that sly wee smirk on your face .
. . that's it . . . Sandy, you've gone too far . . .
Sandy, are you listening? I'm calling my solicitor
. . . I'm calling him now . . . right now . . . it's
ringing . . . he's going to answer in a minute
. . . okay . . . on your own head be it . . . I
tried to be reasonable . . . it's going through
. . . last chance? . . . Ah – oh, hello – could I
speak to my lawyer. please? . . . Steven . . .
Steven . . . son, please . . . yes it's Joe . . . right
away? Thank you – yes, of course I will hold
. . . they're putting me through, Sandy . . . last
chance . . . last chance to apologise, Sandy . . .
he'll pick up any . . .

(JOE's *phone starts to ring loudly.* JOE *gets a fright, drops the phone and then fumbles to recover.*)

Yes? . . . What? . . . No I've not had a fucking accident in the last three years . . . stop phoning me.

(JOE *exits.*)

Day 7

JOE *enters. There is no bench, just a pile of ash and bits of debris. He looks bewildered.* SANDY *enters.*

SANDY   What have you done?

JOE   Hang on a minute, this was nothing to do with me . . .

SANDY   Who was it, then? The Russians? Of course it was you – you're the only sick, homophobic bigot around here who could stoop to such a thing . . .

JOE   I am not homophobic . . .

SANDY   You called me a poof.

JOE   I thought you *were* a poof?

SANDY   There you go again – homophobe – homophobe and now vandal – you vandalised a sacred memorial . . . that's terrorism charges you're facing there . . .

JOE   Don't be ridiculous, and this wasn't me – why would I burn down the bench that I've been fighting to use . . . then turn up again to use it? Cos believe me, if you think your company

was the attraction . . . I'd rather hang out with
ebola-infected estate agents.

SANDY   Are you making jokes again? This is no laughing
             matter – and for the last time, it was not a
             bench – it was a public sacred memorial . . .
             bought and paid for – I have the certificate . . .
             I was applying for National Trust status . . .
             and you – you burnt it to the ground . . . out of
             spite! You're a facist!

JOE   I did nothing of the kind – and I swear to God if
             you call me a fascist again, I'll . . .

SANDY   You'll what? . . . *Punch the poof?* Add assault
             to your list of hate crimes – why not? you've
             already burned a mausoleum to the ground . . .

JOE   It was not the Taj Mahal – it was a fucking
             bench! And I did not set fire to it . . .

SANDY   Liar! You are a liar and a homophobe and a
             vandal and I swear to you now, while there is
             breath left in my body I will fight you and your
             type every step of the way . . .

JOE   What are you talking about? I'm not trying to
             fight you – I didn't do this . . .

SANDY   . . . I will not bow to your tyranny, I will not be
             told to sit down, I will not have my personal
             freedom taken from me and I will – repeat *I will*
             honour the memory of my Maggie . . .

JOE   . . . Maggie was a dog! You would be honouring
             her memory by not pishing on the carpet . . .
             the fact of the matter is – you just don't like the
             idea of this bench belonging to anyone but you
             . . . the fact of the matter is you're just an old
             man who's not very good at sharing . . .

SANDY   . . . It is not a bench, it is a memorial!

JOE   No it's not, Sandy – not anymore – it's a
                       smouldering pile of ash . . . isn't it?

                       (JOE *exits*.)

SANDY   You did this . . . I know it was you . . . this
                       shall not go unpunished . . . there will be
                       repercussions . . . I will honour the memory of
                       my Maggie . . .

Day 8

JOE *arrives.* SANDY *is standing beside a large rectangle, larger than
the bench, covered over with a blanket or sheet. The sign saying
"homophobic prick" is also still visible. There is a portable CD
player also present.*

SANDY   Surprise surprise, I knew you would not be able
                       to stay away from the scene of the crime . . .
                       you're just in time for the unveiling . . .

JOE   I'm here because someone phoned my work
                       and left a message for me to be here . . .

SANDY   That wasn't me.

JOE   (*Reading the message.*) "Tell the homophobic
                       prick to come to the memorial"? . . . My boss
                       read that . . .

SANDY   Nothing to do with me . . .

JOE   You nearly got me fired . . . how did you even
                       know where I worked? . . .

SANDY   I have no interest in talking to you – why would
                       I phone your work?

JOE   Are you following me, Sandy? Are you stalking me?
                       Cos this is starting to get a little bit creepy . . .

SANDY   Stalk you?! You're not my type, son – and
                 why would I need to follow you when where
                 you work is written on that ID badge? . . .
                 And anyway, it wasn't me that phoned – just
                 like it wasn't you that burned down Maggie's
                 memorial . . .

JOE   . . . It wasn't me that burnt down *the bench*.

SANDY   . . . And it wasn't me that phoned your boss, so
                 we're even . . . . but you're here now and you're
                 just in time for the big unveiling . . .

JOE   . . . I know you're gay – I've never had a
                 problem with you being gay . . .

SANDY   Not that – you homophobic prick – of the new
                 memorial – a fitting tribute to Maggie . . . and
                 one that I'm sure you'll be pleased to hear – that
                 I have gone to lengths to make fireproof . . .

JOE   You've replaced the bench? I don't believe it!

SANDY   You will soon see – before the unveiling I would
                 insist on due respect and silence as I play
                 Maggie's favourite song . . . .

                 (SANDY *turns to the portable CD player – Elton
                 John: "I'm Still Standing" comes on –* SANDY
                 *panics and flicks it on to the next track. "The
                 Bitch Is Back" comes on – he finally flicks it on
                 to "Candle in the Wind." They stand solemnly.
                 The track starts to skip – they don't move –
                 Sandy hit's the player with his foot – it jumps
                 back to "I'm Still Standing" . . . he kicks it again
                 it goes back to "Candle in the Wind" – it plays
                 in the background.)*

JOE   Would you just get on with it? . . . I need a
                 seat . . .

SANDY   For those gathered here today . . .

JOE	I'm the only person here . . .
SANDY	. . . To mark the life of Maggie and the impact she made on all of us . . .
JOE	. . . A dog I never met . . .
SANDY	. . . and to commemorate the callous act of spiritual sabotage that was committed on this very spot, not two days ago by unknown homophobic pricks, who are not only intent on desecrating the memory of an innocent but are determined to poison the very spirit of tolerance and acceptance that this country holds as unimpeachable, with their toxic, fascist theology . . .
JOE	. . . Would you buy a full stop!? . . . If you want me to be offended, I need to be awake by the time you've got to the end . . .
SANDY	. . . I – as custodian, as officially recognised by the appropriate council employee responsible – will now unveil the new memorial in commemoration of Maggie . . . a memorial to the memorial if you will . . . I will unveil it now . . . just after a minute's silence . . .
JOE	. . . Right, I've had enough.
	(JOE *pulls the curtain from the memorial. It is a free-standing, large-size mural of the bench*[6] *. . .*)
	You have got to be kidding me!
SANDY	You ruined it! – You ruined the unveiling . . .
JOE	. . . You replaced a bench with a picture of a bench?!

---

6 The more obnoxious and kitsch this picture can be, the funnier the joke. It could include a picture of the dog with wings, flashing lights, etc. . . . go nuts.

SANDY   . . . It's not a *picture of a bench* – it's a public
                 memorial to the first public memorial you
                 destroyed . . . it's a tribute to tolerance . . .

JOE   . . . See, the only problem with that is – you
                 can't actually sit on a tribute to tolerance,
                 can you? I don't think people are going to be
                 feeling that fucking tolerant when they climb
                 all the way up the hill there – get to the perfect
                 spot and instead of a seat, there's a big sod-
                 off picture of a seat – like some kind of shit
                 practical joke – so it's not really a *tribute to
                 tolerance*, is it? It's just a tribute to how much of
                 a twat you are . . .

SANDY   . . . It's a memorial to my Maggie . . .

JOE   Maggie was just a fucking dog! What world do
                 you live in where you think people should give
                 two shits about your dead dog? Have you seen
                 the level of carnage that people manage – on a
                 daily basis – *not* to give a shit about? . . . And
                 you think people should care about this? About a
                 dead Scottie Terrier? . . . If the whole of Scotland
                 was to be nuked out of existence it would barely
                 raise an eyebrow these days . . . half of the UK
                 would applaud[7] . . . I think less of you because
                 you care so much . . . but even more so because
                 you expect other people to . . . need other
                 people to . . .

SANDY   What do you know about loss? Your type – with
                 your entitlement – you'd set fire to the whole
                 world just to draw attention to yourself . . .
                 you'd watch it all burn . . .

JOE   I did not burn it down, Sandy.

SANDY   Then who did, Joe? Who was it?

---

7 Another Scottish reference. This can be changed to *"If the whole of UK . . . and
half of Europe would applaud."*

JOE   . . . In the words of Shaggy – *it wasn't me* . . .

SANDY   Liar.

JOE   Stop it, Sandy. I'm being honest with you . . .

SANDY   You are a liar and a fascist and a homophobic prick.

JOE   Now settle down, Sandy . . .

SANDY   You don't get to tell me to simmer down. I will not take it anymore . . . your mocking . . . I will stand against you . . . you and all your type . . .

             (SANDY *picks up the placard and starts to beat* JOE *with it . . .*)

JOE   Stop it, stop it, Sandy or I'm going to have to . . .

             (JOE *overpowers* SANDY *and restrains him. Beat. All that can be heard is "Candle in the Wind" on a loop.* JOE *starts to laugh, relents his restraint on* SANDY *and sits down. He continues to laugh uncontrollably.*)

SANDY   What's wrong with you? Stop it – stop laughing . . . stop it now.

JOE   . . . *Candle in the Wind* . . .

SANDY   Don't you make jokes about that song, you homophobic prick . . .

JOE   *Candle in the Wind* . . . it was you . . .

SANDY   What do you mean, *it was me?*

JOE   It was you, Sandy – you burnt it down – after you finished with the varnishing – creosote? That was what you used on the bench, wasn't it? Flammable varnish – you put the candles

back on the bench – didn't you? Before it was
properly dry – the varnish caught fire . . . from
the candle . . . in the wind . . .

(JOE *continues to laugh hysterically*.)

SANDY   Stop it, stop laughing . . . this is not funny – that
           is not what happened – you burnt it down – out
           of spite . . .

JOE   . . . You burnt down your own dog's memorial
           with a Candle in the Wind – you're the worst
           gay man ever . . .

SANDY   Stop laughing – this is not funny –

JOE   I beg to differ – you've been calling me a
           homophobe? That's the most anti-gay thing
           you can do, short of assassinating Elton John in
           badly-coordinated camouflage gear . . .

SANDY   Everything is not a joke – that's all this is to you
           – a joke . . . it's not funny – I lost something
           . . . what's funny about that? Why shouldn't I
           want other people to care? I want my loss to
           be marked – I want it recognised . . . logged . . .
           recorded . . . I want there to be something of
           him left in this world . . . something of what he
           meant to me . . . otherwise it was all for nothing
           . . . you're right, you know – I am the worst gay
           man ever . . . you know why it's Maggie's name
           on this and not his? Because I was too scared to
           put his name on it.

JOE   I'm not following . . .

SANDY   She was our excuse – to meet every day –
           Maggie . . . I could never have a dog . . . the
           wife's allergic . . . but the excuse was not for
           my wife . . . she stopped caring decades ago
           . . . if she ever did . . . the excuse was for me
           . . . so I could pretend I wasn't in love with

him – "I'm going to see the dog" – I would tell
myself . . . "spend time with the dog" . . . and
I would walk up here and it always seemed to
me we timed it perfectly . . . he would come up
from the other side at exactly the same time . . .
maybe he waited down there till he heard me
coming . . . it never looked like he was waiting
on me, though . . . Maggie would be first,
barking at me . . . and I would make a show
of petting her . . . like it was her I was here to
see . . . and then when I couldn't hold back for
the wanting of it – only when the anticipation
was at its most exquisitely painful – would I
allow myself to look up at him, look at his face
and . . . (*Beat.*) We would sit together here and
we would talk – mostly about Maggie and we
would watch her running about . . . and then
we would run out of things to say and we would
just sit . . . not saying anything . . . and hours
would go past . . . and then when it was time to
go . . . he'd make a noise . . . always the same
noise – like he was clearing his throat, and he
would lean forward and put his hand on my
knee . . . and I would have to stop myself from
visibly shaking . . . he'd say "thank you for your
company, Sandy," and he would stand up and
put Maggie back on her lead and I would sit
here watching him till he walked away . . . till I
couldn't see him anymore . . . and then I would
stand up and go home . . . and the best part of
my day would be over . . .

(*Beat.*)

JOE   Was that the first time you knew you were gay?

SANDY   Don't be stupid – I've seen more cock in my
             time than most chicken farmers – it was the first
             time I'd ever fallen in love.

JOE   I don't understand . . . but you're married . . .

SANDY   You don't know anything, do you? That's what
               men like me did – march down the aisle with
               the first lesbian you could stomach . . . that was
               the closest we got to Gay Pride . . .

JOE   So did Richard know? . . . Do you think he
               knew . . . how you felt about him? . . .

SANDY   I wish I lived in a world where I didn't know
               the answer to that question.It would be easier if
               there was the possibility that my feelings might
               have been rejected . . .

JOE   He felt the same way? He told you?

               (SANDY *goes into his pocket and pulls out a letter
               that has been read many times. He hesitates
               then hands it to* JOE.)

SANDY   . . . I knew something was wrong that day
               because I heard Maggie from a long way off,
               and it wasn't her usual bark. When I got to the
               bench, I realised she was tethered to it. That
               letter was in a poly bag along with some things
               for Maggie – toys and food and such like . . .

               (*Motions to* JOE *to read . . .*)

JOE   "My dearest Sandy," . . . are you sure I should
               be reading this? . . .

SANDY   Go on . . .

JOE   "My dearest Sandy . . . you'll have guessed I'm
               missing our usual appointment today . . . is
               that what it is? An appointment . . . sounds too
               formal, yet 'liaison' sounds too flirtatious and
               you were never flirtatious, Sandy. Much to my
               disappointment. In truth I should have stopped
               coming some time ago but I guess it's true what
               they say . . . hope springs eternal and I always
               hoped for you, Sandy . . . more than any other

man. I still do, which is why I'm going. I'm
leaving Maggie with you. It turns out I'm not
long for this world and rather than endure the
torture of seeing your yearning turn to pity, I
will bid you adieu in the hope that I will at least
remain beautiful to you. Look after Maggie, and
for crying out loud, allow yourself a little joy,
you miserable old queen. Thank you for your
company, Sandy . . . Love, Richard." (*Beat*.) I
don't know what to say . . . how long ago?

SANDY   Eight months ago.

JOE   Sandy . . . Sandy, I'm so sorry . . . God, this is
               so tragic . . . and then Maggie died? This is the
               saddest thing I've ever heard. When did wee
               Maggie die? . . .

SANDY   About three days later . . .

JOE   Oh Sandy, no . . . that's terrible . . . how did
               she die? . . . Not of a broken heart, Sandy, don't
               tell me that . . . don't tell me the dog died of a
               broken heart . . . I couldn't take that . . .

SANDY   I smashed her head open with a rake . . .

JOE   Fuck sake, Sandy . . .

SANDY   You don't know what it was like . . . after I got
               that note – I hated myself, how could I not?
               There was my one chance of happiness – right
               there in front of me – every day – every day
               for years and I did nothing . . . nothing . . . and
               then it was too late . . . and he was gone . . .
               and all I was left with was a small, needy shit-
               machine constantly barking my mistake at me . . .
               I don't even like dogs . . . and here I was stuck
               with this thing – mocking me day and night – a
               living reminder that if I had been a little braver,
               I may have had something that looked like
               happiness. So as soon as I got home with from

the bench that day, I started drinking and three
nights later, I woke up in my garden with a
rake lying next to me, upon which was impaled
Maggie's head. Not my proudest moment . . .

JOE   Fuck sake, Sandy . . .

SANDY   Obviously I never told them any of this when I
               applied to become custodian . . .

JOE   Fuck sake, Sandy . . .

SANDY   Would you please stop swearing around the
               memorial? . . .

JOE   Your moral outrage is a little less credible after
               the *puppy beheading* anecdote . . . I mean for
               fuck sake . . .

SANDY   You think I don't know it makes me a monster?
               You think I don't know that? . . . How ugly it
               makes me . . . how sorry I am? I never wanted
               to be custodian . . . I hate this place for all the
               same reasons I hated that dog that night . . . but
               it's my penance . . . I force myself to come here
               every day, to remember . . . to remind myself
               just how ugly and stupid I can be . . .

JOE   Fuck sake, Sandy . . . I mean what am I
               supposed to do with that? I don't know what
               any of that means . . .

SANDY   What do you mean you don't know what it
               means? It doesn't mean anything – it's a thing
               that happened . . .

JOE   . . . I mean I don't know what to make of you
               – what to make of any of this. I came here for
               peace, five minutes' peace and I get this . . .
               you're like a horrible riddle I don't want to
               know the answer to – I don't know if you're a
               sad old man who should be pitied or a selfish

old bastard who beats domestic animals to
death with garden implements . . . I mean it's
so unfair . . . this was my place of sanctuary –
my oasis in the shit-storm – and you – you've
destroyed that . . .

SANDY   I've done nothing of the sort.

JOE   Yes you have . . . do you know in all the time
I've been coming here . . . how many days now?
Nine? Ten?

SANDY   Eight.

JOE   Eight then . . . trust you to know that – and in
those eight days . . . not once have you asked
me why I wanted to come here, what this bench
meant to me. Did that even cross your mind?

SANDY   None of my business . . .

JOE   But it *was* your fucking business, as custodian,
surely it was? Did it cross your mind even to
ask? Or were you too intent on trying to cleanse
yourself from the dog massacre . . .

SANDY   So self-indulgent . . .

JOE   Sandy, you turned a public bench into a
testament to your own guilt . . . don't lecture
me on self indulgence . . . you're going to
listen to me . . . not because I think anything
I say will make the slightest difference to you
. . . but because . . . and I can't tell you how
sad this makes me . . . you are the only person
who I can possibly say this to . . . so if the
one outcome of this whole fucked-up story
we've gone through here is that you actually
listen to me, that you do that for me, then
that's something . . . isn't it . . . that would be
a memorial to Maggie and it would mean your

	penance would be over . . . we could both be free of here . . . would that not be a thing? . . .
SANDY	. . . What do you mean? . . .
JOE	I mean, Sandy, I'm offering you a way out, a chance to atone, Sandy, and all you have to do is listen to what I'm about to say, because if I don't say it . . . I don't think I can go on anymore . . .
SANDY	. . . Don't be so dramatic . . . why? Why me?
JOE	. . . Because of this bench, Sandy . . . because of Maggie and Richard, but most of all because I think you know something of how I'm feeling . . .
SANDY	. . . You don't know how I'm feeling . . .
JOE	. . . Okay, I get that . . . I'm not saying that. I'm saying that you might know how I feel . . . and even if you don't . . . that doesn't matter – I just need to say it because if I don't . . . then I might ever not and then . . .
SANDY	And then you might end up like me ? Is that it?
JOE	Bang on the money . . . (*Beat.*) So?
SANDY	And if I do this . . . ?
JOE	You'll be free . . . no more custodian.
SANDY	Say what you have to say.
JOE	Okay . . .
	(*Beat.*)
SANDY	Well go on, then . . .

JOE   . . . Don't rush me . . . this has to be right . . . the
            first time I came here . . . I've not been coping . . .
            that sounds . . .

SANDY   Say what you have to say . . .

            (*SANDY sits down.*)

JOE   . . . This isn't easy . . . okay. The first time I
            came here . . . I didn't mean to come here
            . . . I didn't mean to go anywhere . . . I was
            driving home and I . . . you see there was this
            guy in the office and he hadn't been in for a
            week . . . I mean I'm not that close to him . . . I
            hardly knew him – we weren't friends . . . I just
            knew him said hello to him – anyway, he's not
            been in for a few days . . . and I happened to
            mention it to another colleague and they said
            . . . "Oh, didn't you hear? . . . Colin killed
            himself" . . . like that . . . they just said it like
            that . . . like he had gone on a skiing holiday,
            or . . . and no one had told me . . . and then it
            turned out he had walked out of the office and
            he had walked to a bridge and he threw himself
            off . . . in broad daylight . . . and at the time
            when I heard this . . . I was just kind of numb
            to it . . . but then that night . . . I dreamt about
            him . . . I dreamt that I was standing on the
            bridge and I was the only thing stopping him
            from doing that – from killing himself like that
            – and he was asking me . . . "Why shouldn't I
            do this?" In the dream – he would say – "Give
            me one good reason not to do this . . . just
            one," . . . and I . . . I can't think of anything to
            say . . . and I'm trying . . . I'm racking my brain
            but nothing . . . nothing comes out . . . and he
            walks right past me and he throws himself off
            the bridge.

            And I dreamt that dream night after night until
            it got to the point that during the day I started

trying to think of the reasons I could give him
. . . and I started to look around me and look at
my life . . . not just my life, I mean everything
. . . everything that's happening at the moment
. . . I can't be the only person who feels this . . .
but right now . . . you turn on the news and . . .
I don't understand this world . . . I used to think
that we were progressing . . . the human race,
I mean . . . that the direction of travel was a
positive one, that we were getting better as a
species . . . Is it me? . . . Is it my age? . . . But
I don't think I believe that anymore . . . has it
ever occurred to you . . . that we might be
horrible? People, I mean? . . . That we are just
truly the worst . . . that we're selfish, cruel
beings and that we're not getting any better . . .
we are just more than ever . . . people . . .
because it has occurred to me . . . and when
that occurs to you – its a hard thing to shake,
you know – and that day . . . I pulled over
the car because that is all I could think about
. . . and I had bad thoughts . . . Sandy, I was
thinking of doing something stupid – I had
pills – I don't know what I was going to do but
I intended to something . . . you know . . . and
then I ended up here . . . on this bench . . . and
I broke down . . . right there . . . and I cried . . .
for the first time in years . . . and I felt just a
little bit of peace, just a smidgen of hope and
then I walked back to the car . . . and then I
went home . . .

I came back here, to find that again . . . that
peace – to reclaim it – and instead I get you
. . . you, Sandy . . . and I want to believe that
means something . . . I want to believe that
meeting you was part of a design . . . to teach
me something . . . to bring closure . . . peace . . .
 but you're not going to give me that, are you?
You're not the resolution, cos there isn't one
. . . that's the horrible truth, isn't it . . . we will

never truly know if any of it means anything . . .
so do we just stop trying? Is the most rational
answer to all of this to throw ourselves off a
fucking bridge? Because that seems reasonable
to me – that seems like an appropriate response
to all of this. What would you have said to him,
Sandy? To Colin . . . what reason would you
have given him? What would you have said?
Sandy? . . . Sandy, what would you have said?

(SANDY *doesn't respond.* JOE *notices for the first
time he is slumped, eyes closed.*)

Sandy?

(JOE *runs over, tries to wake* SANDY. SANDY *wakes
with a start.*)

SANDY   Sorry son, I dropped off there . . .

JOE   For fuck sake, Sandy . . . you couldn't stay
           awake for five minutes? . . .

SANDY   . . . Tell us again . . . I'm awake now . . .

JOE   Forget it . . . forget it . . .

SANDY   No – I was listening . . . the dream and that . . .
           about the horse on the bridge . . .

JOE   What horse? There was no horse . . .

SANDY   I'm sure you said something about a horse.

JOE   There was no horse. Just leave it now . . . it's . . .
           it's fine . . .

SANDY   So have I atoned? . . .

JOE   No . . . but you're free all the same . . . go
           home, Sandy . . .

SANDY   Goodbye then, Joe . . .

JOE   Goodbye, Sandy . . .

                         (SANDY *leaves.* JOE *stays still.* SANDY *re-enters
                         awkwardly, without* JOE *seeing him. He looks
                         like he's going to say something, but then just
                         exits again.*)

Day 9

SANDY *enters. He's carrying a portable camping chair and a
newspaper. He also has the sign that used to say "homophobic
prick", but it is turned away from the audience. He sets up his
deck chair in front of the picture of the bench, sits down and
begins to read his paper.* JOE *enters. He is also carrying a portable
chair. He sets it up facing the opposite direction of* SANDY *and
starts to look through his phone.*

SANDY   Did you not bring flowers?

JOE   Thought your penance was over.

SANDY   Aye, but yours isn't . . .

                         (*Beat.*)

JOE   So you just turned up to torment me . . .

SANDY   I haven't the slightest bit of interest in
                         tormenting you . . . I just happened upon here
                         at this time . . . I have every right to be here as
                         much as you . . . some would say more so . . .

JOE   Would they now? Would they indeed? . . .

SANDY   Changed the sign, by the way . . .

JOE   Have you really?

(SANDY *turns the sign around – he's scored out "homophobic".*)

SANDY It just says "prick", now.

JOE I don't believe you . . . do you know that? Let's just not talk . . . let's just sit here in silence . . .

SANDY Say nothing . . .

JOE Quiet contemplation . . .

SANDY Meditate on life . . .

JOE Just stay quiet . . .

BOTH In complete silence . . . shhhhh!

SANDY Fine by me . . .

JOE Fine . . .

(*They both sit silently.*)

(*THE END.*)

Acknowledgements

I would like to thank the following people for their invaluable help with this production; Karen and Katy Koren and all their staff at *The Gilded Balloon* who could not have been more supportive in getting this to the stage. Kenny and Mal and all the staff at *The Stand Comedy Club* who have supported me over the years and allowed me into their beautifully dysfunctional family. To the brilliant Jojo Sutherland and my comedy wife, Paul Sneddon, whose commitment to this play went above and beyond and made doing it such a fucking joy. The *Shambles* Crew – Gus, Robin, Gareth, Pooch (Gareth), Liam, Dave and Larah for their proof reading, friendship and support. To Scott Agnew and Stu Murphy for their wise insight and suggestions in the draft stages. To Richard (Hitch) Hanrahan for the great image. To James Cawood for approaching me during a very busy festival and then making all this happen. To Billy and Patti for that Boxing Day walk and pointing out that bench. To my incredible family for their love, support and tolerance and finally and most importantly to my wife, Jay without whom there would be no reason to write anything as far I'm concerned.